G000270309

BROMLEY SOUTH TO ROCHESTER

Vic Mitchell and Keith Smith

MP Middleton Press

Published November 1993
Reprinted November 2005

ISBN 1 873793 23 5

© Middleton Press, 1993

Design   Deborah Esher
Typesetting   Barbara Mitchell

Published by

    Middleton Press
    Easebourne Lane
    Midhurst, West Sussex
    GU29 9AZ
Tel: 01730 813169
Fax: 01730 812601
Email: info@middletonpress.co.uk
www.middletonpress.co.uk

Printed & bound by Biddles Ltd, King's Lynn

Coverpicture: Class C no. 31713 waits on the down line at Farningham Road on 11th April 1952. After the departure of the up electric on the right, it will run round its two coaches and return to Gravesend West at 3.59pm. (R.C.Riley)

ACKNOWLEDGEMENTS

We are extremely grateful for the assistance received from so many of those mentioned in the captions and also for the help given by R.M.Casserley, D.Collyer, Dr.E.Course, G.Croughton, A.Dasi-Sutton, P.Hay, F.Hornby, T.Heavyside, J.R.W.Kirkby, N.Langridge, A.Ll.Lambert, Mr D. & Dr S.Salter, G.T.V.Stacey, N.Stanyon, R.Randell, C.Wilson and our unceasingly supportive wives.

CONTENTS

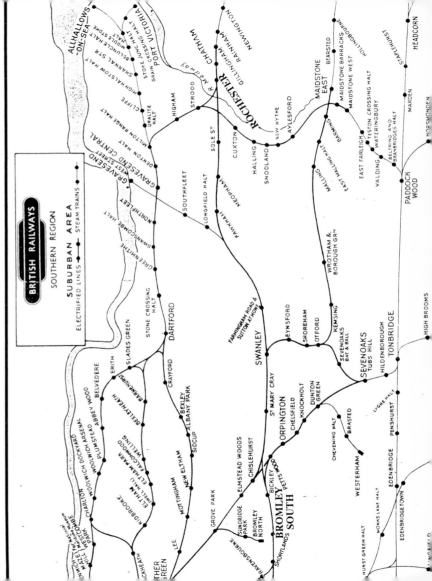

1948 route diagram

GEOGRAPHICAL SETTING

From Bromley to Swanley the line is on an undulating course on the sands of the Blackheath and Thanet Beds. Thereafter the route is mainly on chalk, on which there are a few overlaying patches of gravel which have been of some economic value. This chalk forms the dip slope of the North Downs which is cut through by the River Medway between Strood and Rochester.

The other north flowing rivers crossed by the route are the River Cray at St. Mary Cray and the River Darent at Farningham Road. Both are in deep valleys which help to create the difficult switchback nature of the line.

The descent into the Medway Gap was made less severe by adopting a north-easterly course, although that necessitated a final curve of only 16 chains radius.

The Gravesend West branch makes a steady descent to the south bank of the River Thames. All maps are to the scale of 25" to 1 mile unless otherwise shown.

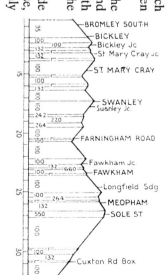

HISTORICAL BACKGROUND

The first line in the area was the London to Strood route which was operated by the South Eastern Railway, opened in 1845 and extended to Maidstone in 1856.

On 21st May 1858 the East Kent Railway Company opened its first line between Rochester Bridge and Faversham. It changed its name to the London, Chatham & Dover Railway in 1859 and embarked on a complicated scheme to reach London, eventually becoming a serious competitor for the SER. Its goal was to link up with the West End & Crystal Palace Railway, which it did by utilising an extension of this line from Norwood to Bromley (now Shortlands), which was opened on 3rd May 1858, together with the Mid-Kent Extension Company's line from Bromley to Southborough Road (now Bickley), which came into use on 5th July 1858. The remaining section between Southborough Road and Rochester Bridge was built by the LCDR and opened on 3rd December 1860, enabling trains to run through to Victoria for the first time.

The LCDR's branch from Sevenoaks Junction (Swanley) to Sevenoaks (Bat & Ball) opened to traffic on 2nd June 1862.

The SER's direct line from London to Tonbridge opened in 1868 and passed over the

LCDR near Bickley. Connections between the two routes were laid down after the SER and the LCDR were united under a joint managing committee in 1899, the combined system soon becoming known as the South Eastern & Chatham Railway. The earlier competitive routes in the Strood/Rochester area are described at the end of this volume, near picture nos. 109 to 111.

The SECR became part of the Southern Railway in 1923.

The branch to Gravesend (West) was an LCDR incursion into SER territory, and came into use on 10th May 1886. It was closed to passengers on 3rd August 1953 but remained open for freight until 25th March 1968.

Electrification of the Bromley South-Bickley section took place on 12th July 1925, when a Holborn Viaduct/Victoria-Orpington service started. The Bickley-Swanley portion received electric trains on 6th January 1935, when Sevenoaks services were modernised. (A thrice-hourly electric service as far as St. Mary Cray ran from 1st May 1934). The part of the route east of Swanley followed on 2nd July 1939 when electric trains were extended to Gillingham.

The lines became part of British Railways upon nationalisation in 1948.

95
100 100
132
132
100
100
100
100
242 220
264
100
100 132 660
100
100 264
132
550
100
100 132
100
660

BROMLEY SOUTH
BICKLEY
Bickley Jc
St Mary Cray Jc
ST MARY CRAY
SWANLEY
Swanley Jc
FARNINGHAM ROAD
Fawkham Jc
FAWKHAM
Longfield Sdg
MEOPHAM
SOLE ST
Cuxton Rd Box
Rochester Bridge Jc

15
20
25
30

PASSENGER SERVICES

Main Line

The following notes refer to down trains and omit express services stopping at two or fewer stations on the route and also trains running on less than five days per week..

The initial timetable had five trains daily. By 1870 the weekday service comprised eleven trains to Rochester or beyond with an additional four to Sevenoaks (Tubs Hill). There were four on the main line on Sundays.

The frequency on the main line in 1890 was 18 as far as Swanley and nine east thereof, with 9 and 4 being the figures on Sundays. The 1910 service had increased to 23 and 11 (12 and 6 on Sundays). Slight alterations brought the 1920 figures to 24 and 14 (15 and 6).

Electrification to Swanley in 1935 brought three trains per hour bound for Sevenoaks (Tubs Hill). East of Swanley, steam trains continued to work the 1930 frequency. The 1940 timetable showed Maidstone East and Gillingham trains dividing at Swanley once in most hours, alternate hours on Sundays. Following the Kent Coast electrification in

1959-61 an hourly local service was maintained but by then Sevenoaks frequency had been reduced to two per hour.

Since May 1976 the basic weekday timetable has had a half-hourly local service on both the main line and the Sevenoaks route, the latter originating at Luton or beyond since 1988.

Gravesend West branch

The initial optimistic service comprised fourteen weekday and eight Sunday trains. Within two years this was reduced to nine and five respectively, up to twelve and seven being common in the years up to World War II.

A daily boat train operated between 1916 and 1939. This semi-fast service from Victoria was available to local passengers.

The 1940 timetable showed only four peak hour trains, with ten on Saturdays and one on Sundays. The 1950 publication indicated three morning and two evening trains (used mainly by workers and scholars), with seven on Saturdays and none on Sundays. A similar service was maintained to the end.

LONDON, SWANLEY, CHATHAM and GILLINGHAM (KENT)

Station rows (Miles from Victoria):

- Victoria .... dep
- Holborn Viaduct .... "
- Blackfriars .... "
- Bromley South ....
- Swanley ....
- Farningham Road A .....
- Fawkham ....
- Meopham ....
- Sole Street ....
- Rochester ....
- Chatham ....
- Gillingham (Kent) .... arr

Section headings: Week Days — Mons only — Week Days (continued) — Sundays

Footnote legend:

A Farningham Road and Sutton-at-Home
E of $ on Saturdays
§ Second class only
# Change at Bromley South
S or $ Saturdays only

† 3 minutes earlier on Saturdays
‡ Second class only
Y 5 minutes earlier on Saturdays
Y 9 minutes earlier on Saturdays

† 14 minutes earlier on Saturdays. Second class only
§ 6 minutes later on Saturdays. Second class only
⊕ Second class only

May 1960

BROMLEY SOUTH

1. The lines were quadrupled in 1893-94 and the station received the suffix "South" on the 1st July 1899, following the formation of the SECR. On the down main line is 0-4-4T R class no. 661 carrying the destination board

BICKLEY MAIN LINE. The large pipe allowed exhaust steam to be condensed while such trains passed through the tunnels to North London. (Lens of Sutton)

2. The horse-drawn pantechnicon seen in the previous photograph is standing on a flat wagon in the dock siding seen more clearly in this later photograph taken on Christmas Day 1938. Prior to the motoring age the carriages of the gentry were sometimes loaded onto such wagons, and attached to passenger trains. (H.C.Casserley)

3. Horse power for coal deliveries was widely employed until about 1950. Coal carts are being loaded as an up train from Gillingham arrives on 5th April 1934, with an oil-lit horse box behind the parcel vans. The locomotive is ex-SER class F1 4-4-0 no. A250. (H.C.Casserley)

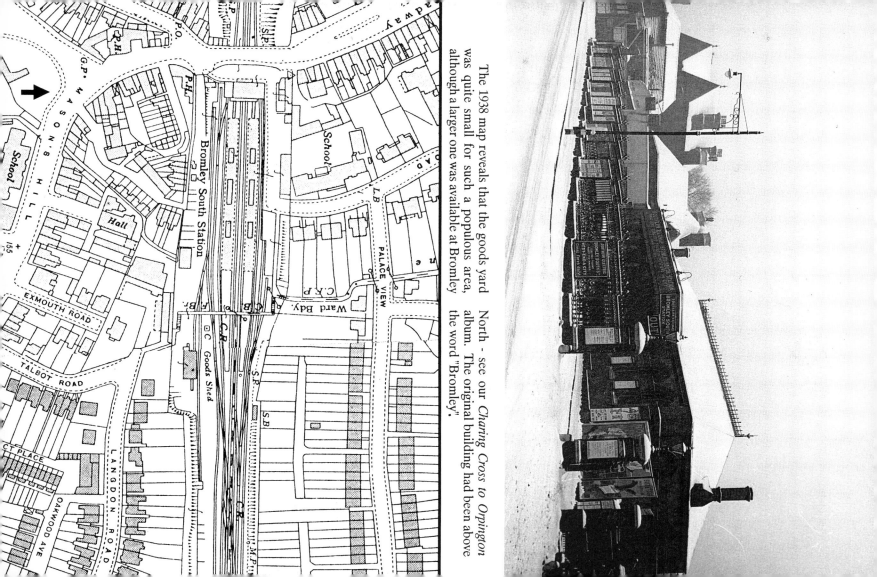

The 1938 map reveals that the goods yard was quite small for such a populous area, although a larger one was available at Bromley North - see our *Charing Cross to Orpington* album. The original building had been above the word "Bromley".

4. The first station building was situated south of the line and was demolished during the quadrupling of the Shortlands-Bickley route. These offices were erected at that time and are seen on Boxing Day 1938. (H.C.Casserley)

5. An eastward view on 22nd October 1932 includes H class no. 1177 on the non-electrified dock siding, and the signal box, which remained in use until 31st May 1959. (H.C.Casserley)

L. C. & D. R.
BICKLEY
TO (S. 24)
BROMLEY
1d. THIRD CLASS 1d.
Available on the day of issue only.
BROMLEY See Other Side
5156

S. E. & C. D. RYS.
BICKLEY
BICKLEY
TO (S. 47)
BROMLEY
1d. THIRD CLASS 1d.
Available on the day of issue only
BROMLEY See Other Side. BROMLEY
2099

6. This is the 1.4pm Victoria-Orpington electric train leaving Bromley South on Saturday, 13th April 1957. The first four-car set is converted from ex-LB&SCR steam stock, while the second set is of post-war SR or BR all-steel construction. (N.Sprinks)

7. As in the previous picture the leading set, albeit 2-car 2HAL, has wooden-framed bodies and a pair of steel coaches follow. Platform widening and lengthening is commencing as a prelude to the 1959 Kent Coast electrification scheme. (F.K.George coll.)

8. The platform extensions are evident as class 5 no. 73085 speeds east with a non-stop relief train on 25th May 1958. Summer holiday rail travel reached its peak that year in most areas. (R.C.Riley)

Other pictures and maps of this station are included in our companion albums *Crystal Palace (High Level) and Catford Loop* and *Victoria to Bromley South.*

9. The Victorian offices were rebuilt and are seen nearing completion on 16th July 1959. Commercial development in the town resulted in two-way peak traffic. Some of the later offices are evident in picture 12.
(British Rail)

10. The spacious new booking hall and an improved all-electric service to London brought increased traffic. Further extensive modernisation took place in 1987, including the provision of energy-wasting sliding doors.
(British Rail)

11. An October 1988 photograph includes the granite setts of the former roadway to the goods yard, which was closed on 19th April 1964. Also included is the second footbridge, which was completed in 1959, and the round-headed windows of 1893 design, which survived the rebuilding. (J.Scrace)

12. Until the 1959 alterations up trains used platforms 1 and 2 (left), but since then they have been allocated 1 and 3. A class 411/5 4CEP occupies the latter on 19th January 1993 and stands under the then recently completed relief road bridge. (M.Turvey)

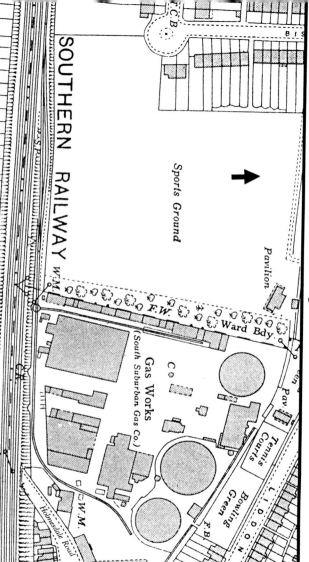

East of Bromley South a trailing connection
(off the left border of this 1937 map) was made
to the gas works siding.

SOUTHERN RAILWAY.
Issued subject to the Bye-Laws,
Regulations & Conditions in the
Company's Bills and Notices.
Day Exc'n as advertised.
Chatham or Rochester to
RICHMOND
Third Class
NOT TRANSFERABLE
SOUTHERN RAILWAY.
DAY EXCURSION.
Richmond
to
Chatham or Rochester
0166

S. E. & C. R. SEE BACK
H. M. FORCES
On Leave in Uniform.
Sevenoaks (T.H.) to
ROCHESTER
Via Swanley Jn.
Third Class 2/1
S. E. & C. R. SEE BACK
H. M. FORCES
On Leave in Uniform.
Rochester to
SEVENOAKS (T.H.)
Via Swanley Jn.
2/1 Third Class
086

SOUTHERN RAILWAY.
PLEASURE PARTY.
County Sanatorium
Available on Day of issue only.
Chatham or Rochester to
BROMLEY SOUTH
Third Class
FOR CONDITIONS SEE BACK
SOUTHERN RAILWAY.
County Sanatorium
Available on Day of issue only.
Bromley South to
LENHAM
Third Class
0056

SOUTHERN RAILWAY.
PLEASURE PARTY.
Available on Day of issue only.
Victoria to
CHATHAM,
GILLINGHAM (KENT)
or ROCHESTER
Third Class. Fare 4/-
SOUTHERN RAILWAY.
PLEASURE PARTY.
Available on Day of issue only.
VICTORIA
CANCELLED
FOR CONDITIONS SEE BACK
Third Class. Fare 4/-
0000

BICKLEY

13. As at Bromley South, the original building was swept away and a new one (of identical design) provided on the road bridge in readiness for the quadrupling. The station opened as "Southborough Road" on 5th July 1858, its name being changed to Bickley on 1st October 1860. (Lens of Sutton)

14. On the left are the remains of the engine shed, a water column, a recess in the wall for another column and heaps of ash. Eight coaches are being accelerated towards London past Bickley "A" box (right) which was in use until 18th July 1926. The shed closed in 1901 when Orpington shed came into use. (Lens of Sutton)

15. SECR cap badges are in evidence as a bowler-hatted inspector gazes upon his bearded station master and assorted clerks. Other ranks are in the back row. There were 31 drivers listed at Bickley back in 1898. (Lens of Sutton)

16. Approaching Bickley is "King Arthur" class N15 no. 772 *Sir Percivale*, displaying experimental smoke deflectors carried in about 1927. The four vestibuled coaches and a van are forming a boat train. (S.A.W.Harvey)

17. The signal box in the background was designated "B" until 1926 and remained in use until 31st May 1959. A bank holiday excursion hurries to the coast on 5th August 1957, class N no. 31405 showing a good clean exhaust. (R.C.Riley)

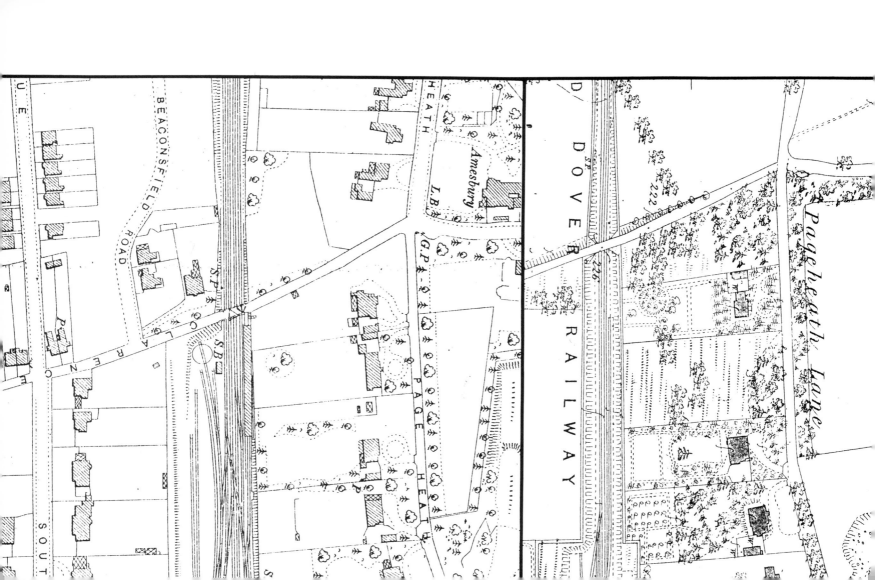

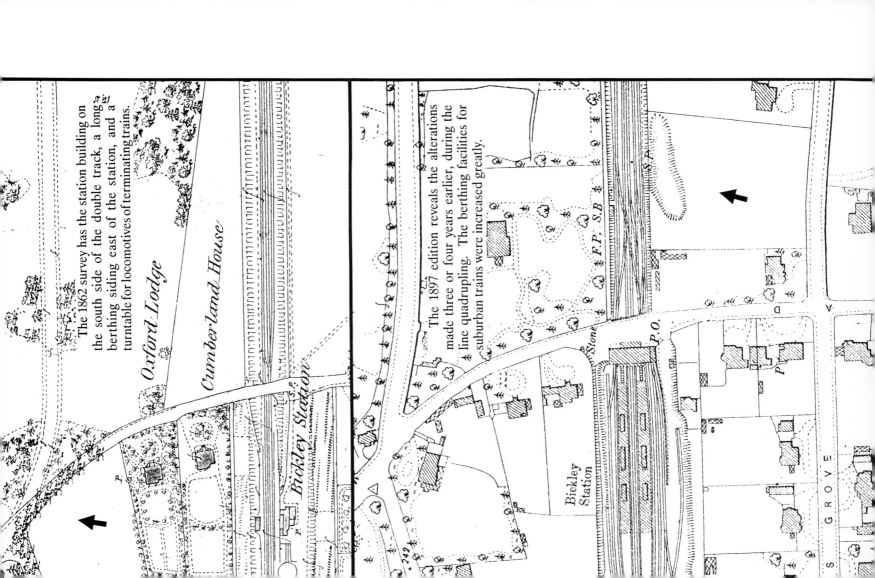

The 1862 survey has the station building on the south side of the double track, a long berthing siding east of the station, and a turntable for locomotives of terminating trains.

Oxford Lodge

Cumberland House

Bickley Station

The 1897 edition reveals the alterations made three or four years earlier, during the line quadrupling. The berthing facilities for suburban trains were increased greatly.

F.P. S.B

S.B.

Stone

P.O.

Bickley Station

GROVE

18. Two 2NOLs stand in the up loop in May 1959, a month before their withdrawal. Their classification indicated that they had - NO Lavatories. (F.K.George)

20. The up relief "Night Ferry" was hauled by class D1 no. 31735 on 13th June 1959, while new 4CEP units wait to go into service (left). The semaphore arms have just been removed and the water tank in the background would not be required much longer. (R.C.Riley)

19. An eastward view from Southborough Road bridge on 6th June 1959 shows the then recently closed signal box and the new track layout. Compare this with picture 17 which was taken from the bridge in the background. (D.Cullum)

22. The 11.47 Dover Western Docks to Victoria races west on 18th January 1990 with MLV no. 9007 leading. These motorised luggage vans were fitted with batteries for working on non-electrified lines, notably in the docks. (J.Scrace)

21. More change was evident on 21st November 1964 as diesel no. D 6563 conveyed nos. 30840 and 30843 (class S15s) to their fate at Queenborough, and the water column awaited removal. Note the ground frame, lower left, which controlled access to the up platform siding. (S.C.Nash)

23. No. 47848 heads the 07.59 Liverpool Lime Street to Folkestone Central on 13th August 1990. This InterCity service called at Bromley South but not Bickley and ran via Dover Priory. In 1993 the train ran on summer Saturdays only and terminated at Dover Western Docks. (J.Scrace)

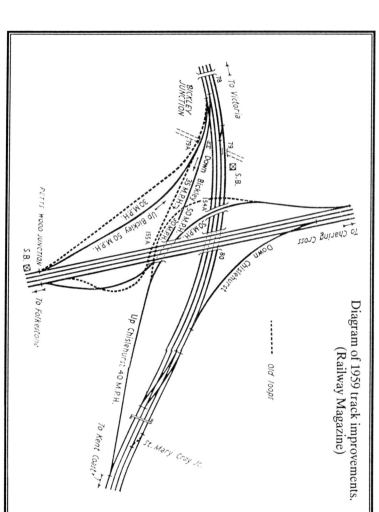

Diagram of 1959 track improvements.
(Railway Magazine)

BICKLEY JUNCTION

On the left of this 6" to 1 mile map of 1910 is the line from Bromley South which was doubled in 1860 and quadrupled in 1894, as far as Bickley. The gas works siding and Bickley station are also shown on this page. From top to bottom is the former SER's 1868 route from St. Johns to Tonbridge. After the formation of the SECR, connections between the routes

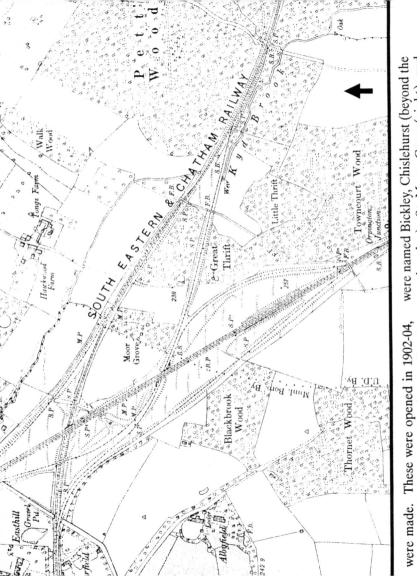

were made. These were opened in 1902-04, the precise dates being given in our *Charing Cross to Orpington* album. The four junctions were named Bickley, Chislehurst (beyond the top border), St Mary Cray (right) and Orpington (renamed Petts Wood in 1936).

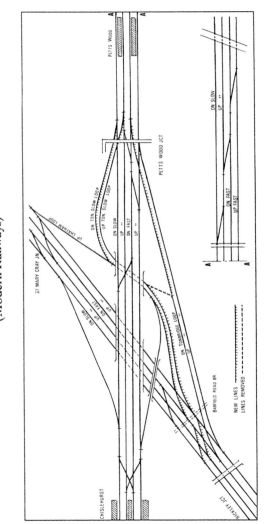

Diagram of 1993 track alterations.
(Modern Railways)

24. The half mile between Bickley and Bickley Junction was quadrupled in 1914. Bickley station is in the distance as we look from Blackbrook Lane bridge on 6th June 1959 at the newly laid connections. (D. Cullum)

25. Looking in the opposite direction, on the same day, we see the then newly quadrupled route to Swanley passing under the ex-SER lines and the Orpington lines on the right. The building in the background once housed rotary converters, machines for converting AC to DC for traction current at a lower voltage. (D.Cullum)

26. A closer view of Bickley Junction box, but at an earlier date, includes 4 SUB no. 4348 working a Sevenoaks to Holborn Viaduct service on 22nd September 1956. The box was in use from 31st May 1914 until the same date in 1959. (R.C.Riley).

27. This box was situated by a level crossing and was replaced by St. Mary Cray Junction Box on 19th June 1904, when the crossing was abolished and the junction was established. (G.D.Metherall)

28. "Schools" class no. 30915 *Brighton* creeps past St. Mary Cray Junction box and the engineering works on 16th May 1959. The train is the 11.30am Ramsgate to Victoria. The quadruple track to Swanley came into use on 31st May of that year when the signal box was demolished. (S.C.Nash)

29. Further major track alterations were in progress when all four Bickley lines were closed on 10th April 1993 in order to increase the junction speeds and improve the layout in preparation for international Eurostar trains, which would run via Swanley or Tonbridge. This westward view includes the 1959 Chislehurst Junction box which since 1983 had only controlled the former SER route and closed completely in April 1993 when Ashford Integrated Electronic Control Centre took over its functions. Only the middle bridge span passed over tracks until 1959. (V.Mitchell)

The 1871 edition at 6" to 1 mile indicates that the small community was gathered along the east bank of the River Cray which provided the power for several mills. The station is on the left, and also evident are the massive embankments which carried the line across the valley.

Brook Wood

U L S S C R

St Paul's Cray

St Mary Cray

LONDON 15 M⁴

ST. MARY CRAY

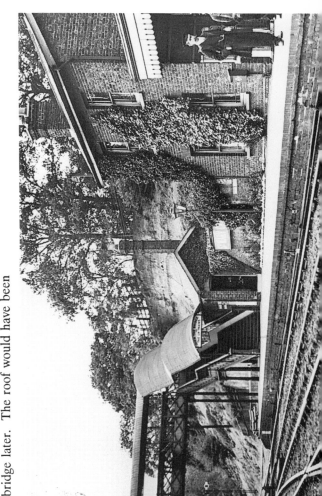

30. An eastward panorama includes the paper mill and the low-set goods shed, which has a roof light. It is recorded that special sidings were provided for unloading London stable manure for use in the numerous market gardens and orchards of the district. (Lens of Sutton)

31. This rural station opened with the line on 3rd December 1860 and was provided with a footbridge later. The roof would have been welcome on occasions at this exposed location. (Lens of Sutton)

32. Ex-LSWR class T9 4-4-0 no. E303 was working the 10.25am Gillingham to Victoria on Sunday 24th December 1933. By then the small canopy had been lost and another up siding gained. (H.C.Casserley)

33. The up platform and down refuge siding were recorded on the same day. Staggered platforms were common on the SER but less so on the LCDR. Geographical considerations probably dictated the arrangement here. (H.C.Casserley)

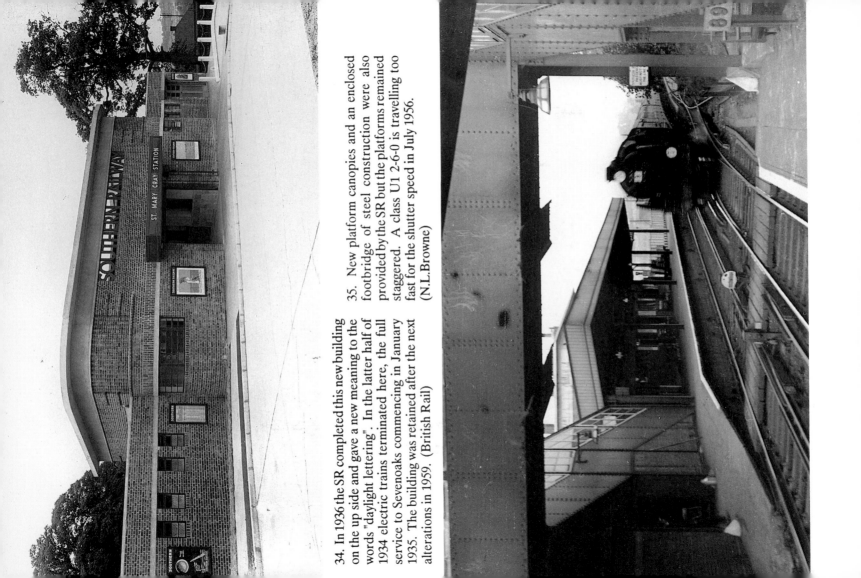

34. In 1936 the SR completed this new building on the up side and gave a new meaning to the words "daylight lettering". In the latter half of 1934 electric trains terminated here, the full service to Sevenoaks commencing in January 1935. The building was retained after the next alterations in 1959. (British Rail)

35. New platform canopies and an enclosed footbridge of steel construction were also provided by the SR but the platforms remained staggered. A class U1 2-6-0 is travelling too fast for the shutter speed in July 1956. (N.L.Browne)

The 1909 survey marks the viaduct that linked the two embankments and spanned the river and mill race. The signal box (S.B.) on the left was designated "A" and closed on 24th October 1926.

The 1937 map shows that the expansion of the up sidings involved massive earthworks and that the former orchard on the south side was used to provide access to the new buildings.

Church Hill

Station

Station

Station Square

Goods Shed

Goods Shed

AMHERST CRESCENT

H RISE

S.B.

S.P.

S.P.

W.M.

L.B.

F.P.

P.F.

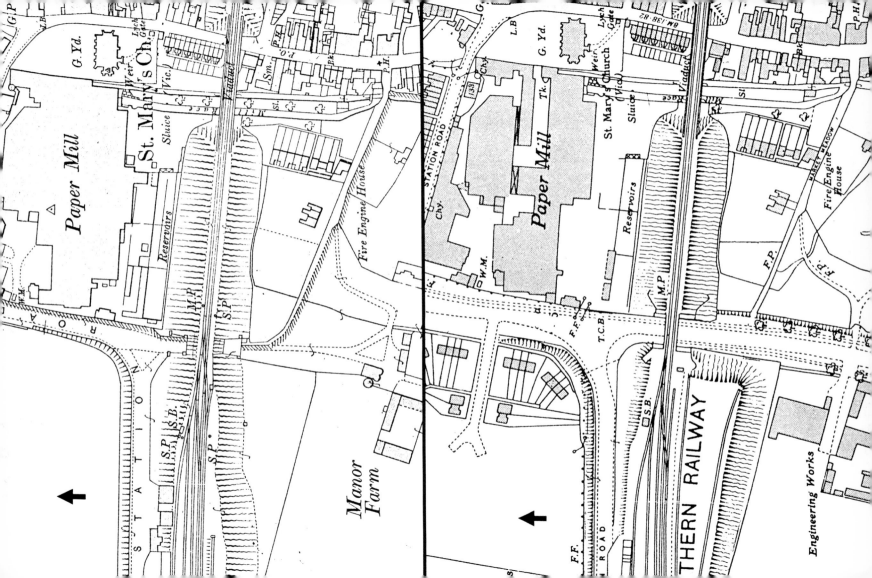

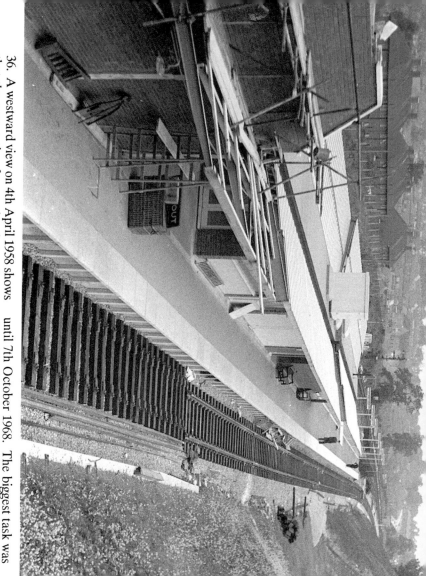

36. A westward view on 4th April 1958 shows that the new station for quadruple track was well advanced. The developments did not affect the goods yard which remained in use until 7th October 1968. The biggest task was the widening of the nine-span viaduct with brick piers and reinforced concrete arches. (N.L.Browne)

37. The station was complete as no. D5001 (later no. 24001) runs towards London on 9th May 1959, three weeks before the semaphore signalling and signal box were taken out of use and the two extra tracks were commissioned. Sixteen of these type 2s were borrowed from the LMR while delivery of class 33s was awaited. (R.C.Riley)

38. Working an up service from Sevenoaks on 2nd September 1959 is one of the first generation of EMUs which were first assembled as 3-car sets. After WWII many were augmented with a fourth coach, often a wider all steel one, as seen near the new wider footbridge. (R.C.Riley)

39. The 09.25 Dover Priory to Victoria passes the 10.00 Luton to Sevenoaks on 1st October 1992. Such Thameslink services began to serve the Bromley South - Swanley part of the route in May 1988 giving direct travel to Kings Cross and other destinations in North London. (J.Scrace)

40. Kevington Box was less than a mile from St. Mary Cray and had ceased to be used by 1922. (G.D.Metherall)

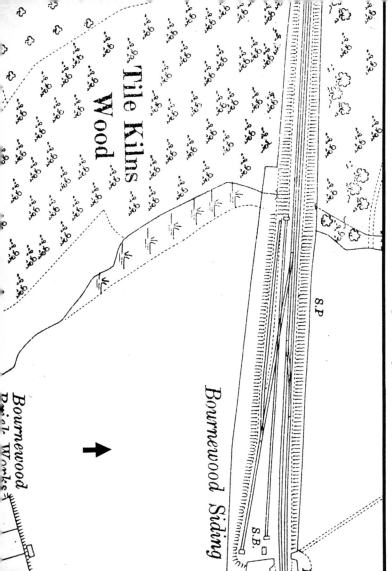

Tile Kilns Wood

S.P

Bournewood Siding

S.B.

Bournewood Brick Works

L. C. & D. R.

ST. MARY CRAY
ST. MARY CRAY (3. 11)
TO

SWANLEY

THIRD CLASS 3d.

3d. Available on the day of issue only
See Other Side. SWANLEY

SWANLEY

8006

8006

The next box east is marked on this 1933 map and was listed as "Bournewood Crossing". It was superseded by automatic semaphore signals on 1st July 1934. The sidings were still in use in 1938, the nearby brickworks no doubt generating traffic for them.

SWANLEY

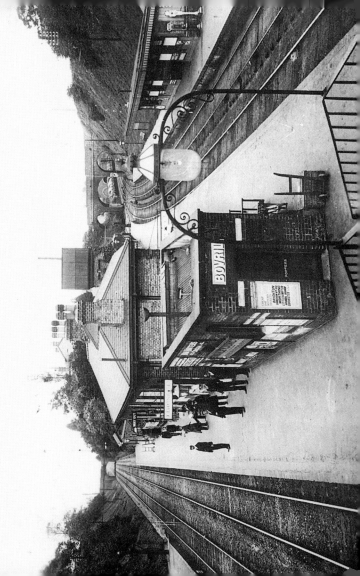

41. The station opened on 1st July 1862 as "Sevenoaks Junction", the day on which the branch to that town came into use. The name was changed to "Swanley Junction" on 1st January 1871, the suffix being dropped on 16th April 1939. (Lens of Sutton)

42. While the platform arrangement was suitable for the steam era and branch line operation, the advent of electrification and the need to divide and join trains necessitated a new station. (Lens of Sutton)

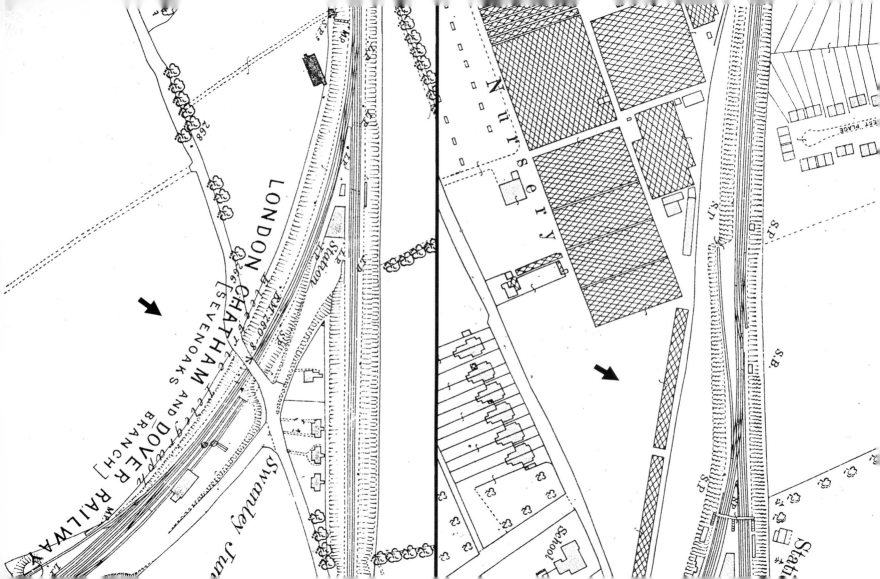

LONDON CHATHAM [SEVENOAKS AND DOVER BRANCH] RAILWAY

Swanley Junction

Station

Nursery

School

S.P.

S.B.

Station

EST PLACE

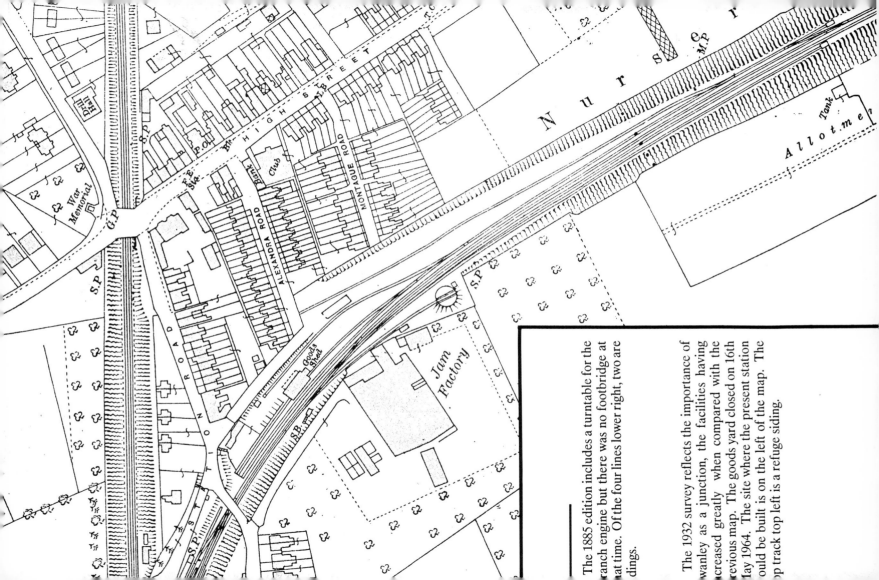

The 1885 edition includes a turntable for the
branch engine but there was no footbridge at
that time. Of the four lines lower right, two are
sidings.

The 1932 survey reflects the importance of
Swanley as a junction, the facilities having
increased greatly when compared with the
previous map. The goods yard closed on 16th
May 1964. The site where the present station
would be built is on the left of the map. The
top track top left is a refuge siding.

43. The 11.8am Holborn Viaduct to Gilling-ham waits to depart behind class D no. 1731 on 12th November 1938. Some platform canopies have appeared since the last photograph was taken. The station master's house (the nearest one) was still standing in 1993.
(H.C.Casserley)

44. Another photograph from the same day includes the gallows style down starting signal, conductor rails ready to position and both old and new signal boxes. The water column was supplied by the tank seen in pictures 41 and 42.
(H.C.Casserley)

45. A closer look at the boxes that day shows work in progress to widen the cutting to accommodate the new station which is being built beyond the new box. Slip coaches were shed from down expresses in 1872-99 and in 1914-24. (H.C.Casserley)

46. The area on the left of the previous picture had earlier been the site of an accident involving class L no. 1768 on 27th June 1937. Two days later its tender wheels were being removed, while it lay on its side under sheets like a corpse. The driver of the 8.17pm Margate to Victoria via Maidstone East had been confused by the signal alterations and collided with a motor train standing in the siding, pushing it into the switching station. There were four fatalities and eleven serious injuries. (H.C.Casserley)

47. A down train (Maidstone East via Catford Loop) arrives on 29th May 1959 on what would become an up line the following week, by which time the trackwork in the background would have been altered and mechanical signalling discontinued. A coal dues obelisk was still situated in 1993 near the right fence in the far distance. A Metropolitan coal tax was levied until 1890. (J.J.Smith)

48. Recorded on the same day is "Schools" class no. 30912 *Downside* working the 6.14pm from Cannon Street which was due at Ramsgate at 8.23. Its first stop was at Whitstable. (J.J.Smith)

49. An eastward view on the same day reveals that the old station buildings and water tank were still standing in the fork of the junction. The signal box closed on 19th June 1983 when control of the area was transferred to Victoria Panel. (J.J.Smith)

50. The former station site was very overgrown when no. 33033 roared west with a stone train on 28th June 1992. Extensive engineering work was undertaken in Kent that year in readiness for the opening of the Channel Tunnel in 1994. (M.J.Stretton)

51. The unimposing entrance leads to a small booking hall which is on the same level as the footbridge. Seen in 1992, this building replaced temporary huts which were erected pending a decision on the route of Swanley bypass, which might have crossed the line west of the platforms. (J.Scrace)

FARNINGHAM ROAD

52. The main sign on the down platform reads "Farningham Road & Sutton at Hone", a name adopted in January 1872 after a number of changes. The other sign declares "Station for Homes for Little Boys Farningham". For some years from 1870 this home had its own platform further east, on the down side only. Lads from the poorer parts of London arrived at the home and were eventually distributed to training ships - hence no up platform. After the water tank was removed, the brick building was converted to a waiting room. (Lens of Sutton)

53. A view towards London in the summer of 1921 shows alterations and platform raising in progress. Although the junction for the Gravesend West branch, no bay platform was provided. For many years branch trains operated to and from Swanley Junction. From January 1910 they were for long worked by P class 0-6-0T no. 323, now on the Bluebell Railway. (H.J.Patterson Rutherford)

54. Refuse from London was (and still is) a good source of railway revenue. The wagons on the left are destined to Longfield siding with rubbish. They had to be stood remote from dwellings on account of their smell and resident fly population. This up train on 21st May 1938 is headed by class D 4-4-0 no. 1075. (H.C.Casserley)

55. Recorded on the same day is the 2.05pm push-pull train from Gravesend West, propelled by class R 0-4-4T no. 1669. This was a Saturdays-only service which terminated here. On the right is the 1.35 (SO) Victoria to Sheerness-on-Sea. (H.C.Casserley)

56. Push-pull working was ideal at this location since running round obstructed the main lines, as witnessed on the cover of this book. Having just used the crossover in the foreground, class R no.31662 is entering one of the two sidings on 21st April 1953. (R.C.Riley)

57. The coal yard is seen from the footbridge on 11th August 1956 as class 5 4-6-0 no. 73080 *Merlin* speeds towards London. Freight facilities were withdrawn on 20th May 1968. In the background the line drops at 1 in 100 into the Darent Valley and climbs out at 1 in 100. (A.E.Bennett)

M.P. London 20

Farningham Road Station

58. In 1985 the Venice Simplon Orient Express stock was used for a number of circular tours of Kent. On 2nd July 1985 it was hauled by electro-diesel no. 73123 *Gatwick Express*, seen here with shoes down and diesel engines switched off. (J.S.Petley)

SOUTHERN RAILWAY.
N. S. L. Half-Day Excursion.
Available as advertised.

Bromley South to

Bromley South
Herne Bay or Whitstable
HERNE BAY or WHITSTABLE
& TANKERTON and BACK

Bromley South
Herne Bay or Whitstable

THIRD CLASS   THIRD CLASS

FOR CONDITIONS SEE BACK

7678   7678

This early map is from about 1885 and has the unusual feature of a crane alongside the main line. It should be "water crane" (for locomotives). The footpath starting near it gave direct access to Sutton-at Hone.

Farningham R Statio

Chalk Pit

S.P.

Crane

Goods Shed

F.P.

S.B.

S.P.

L.B.

The 1909 survey marks a crane which was of 5-ton capacity. This was the only intermediate station on the route to have anything more than a 30cwt goods shed crane.

59. The 13.11 Victoria to Ramsgate pulls in on siding for the steel stockholder was closed in 13th October 1992, its schedule showing a call September 1980 and the signal box followed on at all stations east of Bromley South. The 12th June 1983. (J.Scrace)

60. The exterior was little altered when photographed in 1992. Between 1909 and 1914 the station had witnessed a weekday down slip coach operation. In 1910 this was off the 5.36pm from Victoria at 6.13, the slipped portion continuing at 6.19, all stations to Chatham. (J.Scrace)

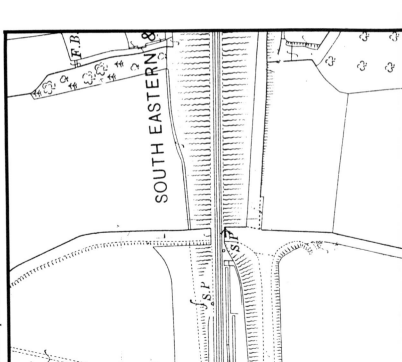

0354
SOUTHERN RAILWAY.
CONVALESCENT HOME.
Available for Three Months,
including Day of Issue & return.
Herne Bay to
BROMLEY SOUTH
Third Class
FOR CONDITIONS SEE BACK
SOUTHERN RAILWAY.
CONVALESCENT HOME.
Available on Day of issue only.
Bromley South to
HERNE BAY
Third Class
Not available unless
dated before use.
0354

SOUTH EASTERN &
F.B.
F.P.
S.P.
S.P.

61. The Gravesend West branch drops away from the mainline at 1 in 100, this rising at 1 in 132 from the junction. The box closed on 10th May 1959 after which date the points were controlled remotely from a small panel in Farningham Road box. The sub-station is also included in this photograph from February 1952. (D.Cullum)

ills Wood

F.F.

SOUTH EASTERN & CHATHAM RAIL

TRAMWAY

S.P.

S.B.

[108]   LONDON, ROSHERVILLE, and GRAVESEND.—London, Chatham, and Dover.

Down.

Fares from Victoria,
Holborn Viaduct, Ludgate
Hill, or St. Paul's.

SINGLE.   RETURN.

1 cl. 2 cl. 3 d. 1 cl. 2 cl. 3 d.
s. d. s. d. s. d. s. d. s. d. s. d.

Victoria...............dep
Clapham & N.S. "
Briton & S.S. "
Holborn Viaduct
Ludgate Hill "
St. Paul's "
Borough Road "
Elephant & Castle "
Walworth Road "
Camberwell N. Rd. "
Loughboro' Jnc. "
Herne Hill "
Dulwich "
Sydenham Hill "
Penge (Beckenham) "
Kent Ho. (Beckenham) "
Beckenham "
Shortlands "
Bromley "
Bickley "
St. Mary Cray "
Swanley Junction "
Farningham Rd. "
Southfleet "
Rosherville "
Gravesend 101 "

SUNDAYS.

[Fares.]   GRAVESEND, ROSHERVILLE, and LONDON.—London, Chatham, and Dover.

Up.

SINGLE.   RETURN.
1 cl. 2 cl. 3 d. 1 cl. 2 cl. 3 d.

Gravesend.............dep
Rosherville. "
Southfleet* "
Farningham Rd. "
Swanley Jnc 101 "
St. Mary Cray "
Bickley "
Bromley "
Shortlands "
Beckenham 86, 104, "
Kent House (Beck.) "
Penge (enham) "
Sydenham Hill "
Dulwich "
Herne Hill 41, "
Loughbro' Jn. arr
Camberwell N.R. "
Walworth Rd. "
Elephant & Castle "
Borough Road. "
St. Paul's "
Ludgate Hill. "
Holborn Viaduct "
Briton & S.S. arr
Clapham & N.S. "
Victoria 4, 191 "

SUNDAYS.

* Station for Springhead.
a. Gravesend Cheap Trains.
† Farningham Road and Sutton-at-Hone.

February 1890

The 1909 map gives an unofficial name to the junction and also includes a private siding with its associated narrow gauge line to a gravel pit. On the left is part of Wood's siding.

Pinden

Pinden Junction

S.P   S.B   S.P

Gravesend West branch

The 1930 map at 1" to 1 mile shows that Fawkham station was in Longfield and that Longfield Halt was about half a mile to the north. The branch was nearly five miles long and is shown in its entirety. Watling Street was upgraded for the use of motor vehicles in 1924 and the former occupation crossing replaced by a girder bridge over the road, which was designated A2. An additional span was erected when the road was widened in 1965.

LONGFIELD HALT

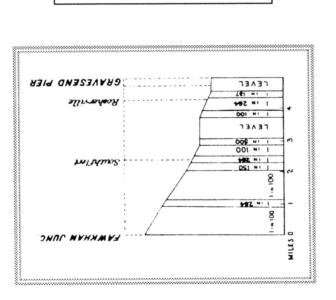

£000
SOUTHERN RAILWAY.
RAIL MOTOR CAR.
Available only for any journey
(in either direction.)
To be shown on demand.

THIRD CLASS SINGLE
Fare 3½d

(A) BETWEEN
LONGFIELD HALT
AND
SOUTHFLEET

This ticket must be punched
opposite the Junction or Halt
to which the Passenger is
entitled to travel.

FOR CONDITIONS
SEE BACK

62. Two wooden platforms with identical waiting shelters came into use on 1st July 1913. The down platform is seen with a generous covering of chalk in September 1952. (J.H.Aston)

63. A damp and gloomy day in February 1951 was not the best occasion on which to record such details as the loading gauge and the protective barrier around the ground signal. The heap of sacks is a reminder that railway companies once offered a sack hire service to their customers. Staffing ceased in 1953. (D.Clayton)

The 1933 map indicates the extent of the sidings and position of the staff dwellings. A trailing siding for Chambers was provided from the down line about a mile to the south until 10th August 1964. The North Downs Steam Railway Society launched a preservation scheme at this location in July 1980, but had to abandon it in April 1983. Success was achieved at Stone, near Dartford.

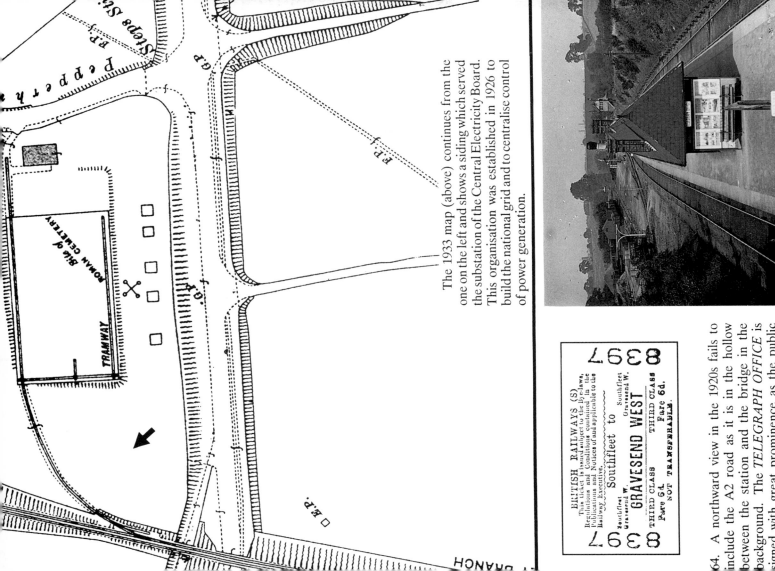

The 1933 map (above) continues from the one on the left and shows a siding which served the substation of the Central Electricity Board. This organisation was established in 1926 to build the national grid and to centralise control of power generation.

64. A northward view in the 1920s fails to include the A2 road as it is in the hollow between the station and the bridge in the background. The *TELEGRAPH OFFICE* is signed with great prominence as the public telegraph service was a considerable source of revenue. (H.J.Patterson Rutherford)

65. The box controlled a crossover a little to the north of it, and another south of the road bridge. In its final years it was simply a ground frame controlling access to the goods yard. (J.H.Aston)

66. The 3.59pm from Farningham Road was hauled by class R no. 31671 on 11th July 1953, only three weeks before closure. The goods yard remained open for traffic until 11th June 1962 and despatched large quantities of soft fruit in the season. (S.C.Nash)

67. The RCTS "London & North Kent" railtour visited the branch on 21st March 1959, headed by class E1 no. 31507. The tour started at Liverpool Street (hence Eastern Region coaches) and ran via Cannonbury, East Finchley, Farringdon, Nunhead, Eltham, Lee, Chislehurst and Swanley to Gravesend West. Return was via Hither Green and the East London Line, five different locomotives being used during the day. The last railtour on the branch was on 3rd March 1968, the LCGB "Invicta". (S.C.Nash)

68. The lamp remained in place at the top of the steps after passenger services were withdrawn and long after the SR had ceased to exist. An attempt was made in 1984 by Resco (Railways) Ltd to establish a railway museum but after failure the track north to the A2 was lifted for re-use on the Kent & East Sussex Railway. The A2 bridge was demolished in 1992. (J.H.Aston)

69. Life returned to the slumbering outpost on 21st November 1959 when a group of enthusiasts arrived on a down freight, a second brake van being provided for their benefit. Pylons and chimneys have encroached on the skyline since picture 63 was taken and the site was subsequently used by a road haulage firm. (J.J.Smith)

The diagram indicates the layout after the southern part of the branch was reopened for coal traffic to the APCM local cement mills. The terminal was in use from 1972 to 1976 and was provided with a Sentinel 0-4-0 diesel for shunting. Coal came from the Midlands (behind LMR locomotives) and from Tilmanstone Colliery in Kent and was forwarded by road.

Engine Shed

Tippler

Tramway Depot

Allotments

P.H.

TRAMWAY

S.P.

M.P.

PROPOSED CONNECTION

50·70

52·00

71·63

24·76

19·66

GRADIENT 1 IN 40

MILL ROAD

TO BRICKFIELD

Tunnel

DUDLEY ROAD

Allotment Gardens

Chalk Pit

The 1909 map has the North Kent
ne running diagonally to the top
ght towards Gravesend, whereas our
ute runs from bottom to top. The
amway is that of the Gravesend,
osherville and Northfleet Tramway
ompany, horse-worked from 1881,
ectrically from 1902-03 and closed in
29. The "proposed connection" was
er laid down to serve Bowater's
per mill and from another private
ing a line ran for one mile to the
ritish Portland Cement Works at
orthfleet. Near the top of the map is
two-road engine shed which was
tle used after the introduction of
otor train working in 1910. It closed
the 1920s.

70. The branch passed over the electrified North Kent line on a skew bridge. A power cable ran from near here to the sub-station seen in picture 61. Plans for a high speed link between London and the Channel Tunnel envisage track being relaid on the southern part of the branch to provide a link between it and the existing main line at Fawkham Junction. (A.E.Bennett)

71. The train seen a few minutes earlier in picture 69 has arrived at Perry Street sidings with class C 0-6-0 no. 31682 more obvious. The bridge is at the top of the map. The branch had been singled in 1959 but a loop was retained at Southfleet. (J.J.Smith)

ROSHERVILLE

72. The main building at Rosherville was at the road level and was approached by a U-shaped drive which was fairly overgrown when recorded in September 1952. (J.H.Aston)

73. Traffic was so light that staffing ceased on 17th June 1928, an early example of a practice common in the 1990s. Closure was also at an early date - 16th July 1933. (R.Carpenter coll.)

Vicarage

Rosherville Station

S.B.

M.P.

TRAMWAY

BURCH ROAD

Lodge

Lodge

Hotel

F.S.

Rosherville Pier
(Disused)

LANSDOWNE SQUARE

PIER ROAD

F.W.

Und.

SLAVES ALLEY

F.S.

Wharves

Bycliffes

Gridiron

Lodge

S.P.

P.H.

S. E. & C. PIE[R]

Dolphin ○

○ *Dolphin*

○ Dolphin

M u d

M u d

Commercial Cr.

Brewery

CLIFTON

F.S.

S.P.

Wharf

Coal Wharf

Baltic Wharf

Timber Yard

Gridiron

Causeway

New Thames Yacht Club Ho.

Clifton Baths (Disused)

MARINE PARADE

F.S.

P.H.

Lime Works

S.P.

S.P.

S.P.

S.B.

Station

W.M.

W.M.

Goods Shed

Cattle Pens

Cr.

S.P.

Whiting Works

STUART ROAD

Timber Yd.

BLIGH ROAD

Hospital

Public Hall

School

St. James's Ch.

ST. JAMES'S STREET

Institute

Technical Institute

ST. JAMES'S ROAD

S.B.

Statue

P.H.

S.P.

S.P.

Rifle Range

Targets

100

50

66

100

200 Yds.

The 1909 edition has Rosherville station lower left and part of Rosherville Gardens top left. The latter was a popular recreational venue from 1840 until 1900, most visitors from London arriving by Thames steamer. They reopened in the period 1903-10 but tastes were changing. No doubt the LCDR helped to carry some of the 14000 pleasure seekers on the Whit Monday of 1886. The map shows three bridges over the 3ft 6ins gauge lines of Tolhurst & Sons Ltd. The site was later used for the Imperial Paper Mills and a trailing siding was laid near Gravesend West Street station, which is shown top right. The approach to Gravesend Central is lower right.

74. Class R no. 31662 nears the end of its journey on 25th April 1953, leaving the fine tracery that had not been admired by passengers for 20 years. At this period this class of locomotive generally only appeared on the branch for the augmented Saturday service. (J.J.Smith)

2941

L.C. & D.R.
ROSHERVILLE
TO
FARNINGHAM ROAD
THIRD CLASS 6¼d.
6¼d.
Available on the day of issue only.
See other Side.
FARNINGHAM RD.
FARNINGHAM

2941

5029

SOUTHERN RAILWAY
This Ticket is issued subject to the Company's Bye-laws, Regulations and Conditions in their Time Tables, Notices, and Book of Regulations.
Gravesend W. St.
Longfield Halt
Gravesend West St. to
LONGFIELD HALT
Gravesend W.St
Longfield Halt
THIRD CLASS
Fare 6d.
THIRD CLASS
Fare 6d.

5029

75. The covered footbridge linked the back of the building seen in picture 72 with the two flights of steps to the platform. Class R 0-4-4T no. 31671 drifts down the gradient towards the terminus on 11th July 1953, working the 5.13pm from Farningham Road. (S.C.Nash)

76. The freight capacity at Gravesend Central was very limited and so the facilities at Gravesend West were retained, goods trains rumbling through the deserted platform until 1968. The station master's house is above the locomotive. (Lens of Sutton)

GRAVESEND WEST

77. On the right is the local train while on the left is a boat train composed of corridor coaches with roof boards. The Batavier Line operated a service to Rotterdam from the pier between 1916 and 1939. "Batavier" was the spelling used by the SR but "Batavia" was to be found elsewhere. The date is 11th June 1938 and the boat train engine is C class 0-6-0 no. 1576. (H.C.Casserley)

78. The station was simply "Gravesend" until June 1899 when "West Street" was added. The "Street" was dropped on 26th September 1949. The new sign was photographed on 20th September 1952 as class H no. 31295 was about to depart at 3.4pm. This class largely superseded the Rs in the final years. (J.H.Aston)

79. Two locomotives were present on 11th April 1953 as the photographer included in the panorama the signal box, the cattle pens, the goods shed, the water tower and the turntable. (R.C.Riley)

80. A close up on the same day shows a local train in the shorter platform. This was 427ft. long which compares with 526ft for the other. Maidstone & District buses are parked in the goods yard. (R.C.Riley)

81. Empty Eastern Region stock leaves behind class N no. 31857 and is bound for Grove Park on 25th April 1953. Two of the bridges that once spanned narrow gauge lines are evident. Passenger services ceased on the branch on 3rd August 1953. (J.J.Smith)

82. This sign was still visible in July 1953 at which time the General Steam Navigation Company's *Royal Daffodil* called at this pier throughout the summer. (R.C.Riley)

JUNE 1953 DEPARTURES	
Mon-Fri	Saturday
am	pm
6.54S	12.55F
7.50S	1.48F
pm	3.04F
4.50F	4.46F
6.42S	6.03F
8.00S	7.25F
	8.35S
	9.50C

No Sunday service
S to Swanley
F to Farningham Road
C to St. Mary Cray

JULY 1926

SOUTHERN RAILWAY
GRAVESEND WEST STREET
STATION

THE SOUTHERN RAILWAY CO.,
HEREBY GIVE NOTICE THAT
IN PURSUANCE OF THE POWERS
VESTED IN THEM, A CHARGE OF
1/3 WILL BE MADE IN RESPECT
OF EACH PASSENGER EMBARKING
OR DISEMBARKING AT THIS
PIER.

BY ORDER

83. Three years after passenger service ceased the poster was inviting you to park your car at a charge of one shilling. Maybe this facility was used by the Tilbury Ferry users. In the early years many passengers travelled via Tilbury, as the rail fare was almost half north of the Thames. The short platform was through the left arch. The approach road was V-shaped. (N.L.Browne)

84. Shunting the yard on 21st November 1959 was C class no. 31682. By then there was only one track to the turntable. The disused chalk quarry is in the background. (J.J.Smith)

85. Other details recorded on the same day include the Imperial Paper Mills siding (beyond the van on the right) and the "TO THE

BOATS". Some signs were thoughtfully written in Dutch as well. (J.J.Smith)

86. As at the main line stations in this volume, the goods shed contained a crane of 30cwt capacity for general merchandise. In the goods yard (and marked on the map Cr.) was one of 10-ton lifting power. (C.Hall)

88. The roofs seen in picture 83 appear again behind the buildings on platform 1. The Batavier Line ships departed from the Pool of London (between Tower and London Bridges) and called here to embark passengers who had left Victoria much later by train. (J.J.Smith)

89. Viewed from the coal fired paddle steamer Kingswear Castle on 3rd August 1992, the railway pier stood out like a sore thumb (or bruised one, being backlit by the evening sun). Plans to create a resturant on it had not materialised. (V.Mitchell)

87. No. 1 platform connected with the covered walkway on the pier, shown in 1959. The road bridge (foreground) and the pier were still in situ in 1993 awaiting their fate. Tilbury is in the background - it lost its Riverside station in November 1992. (J.J.Smith)

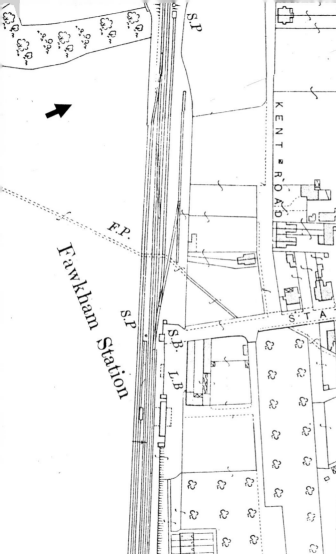

LONGFIELD

90. Although situated adjacent to Longfield, the station was named Fawkham until 12th June 1961, When the station opened, in June

1872, the population of the former was only 188 and the latter was 233. The combined figure for 1921 was only 1163. (Lens of Sutton)

The 1909 survey indicates two down goods sidings and one up refuge siding, a plan that did not change subsequently.

91.   Another view of the down platform includes the small goods yard which was in use until 7th May 1962. These two photographs show ballast over the sleepers, a practice to be banned owing to the difficulty in detecting defective sleepers. (Lens of Sutton)

92. An up goods train rattles down the 1 in 100 gradient which levelled briefly through the platforms. C class 0-6-0 no. 1686 is in charge on 20th May 1936, assisted by the guard in the brake van. Continuous brakes on goods trains were then rare. (H.C.Casserley)

93. A 1959 eastward panorama includes the long up refuge siding, the footbridge extension (right) which connected with a public footpath, and the signal box which was taken out of use on 28th November 1965. It had controlled colour lights since 1959. The building on the left was not railway property. (D.Cullum)

94. When pictured on 1st October 1992 the former goods yard had become the inevitable car park, and the station approach had been subjected to commercial development. This is the 14.11 Victoria to Ramsgate which is worked by unit no. 3162 fitted with the then new warning light. (J.Scrace)

95. The historic station building with its charming and unusual vaulted canopy was swept away in favour of this featureless structure of CLASP design, which was not even maintenance free. (J.Scrace)

LONGFIELD SIDING

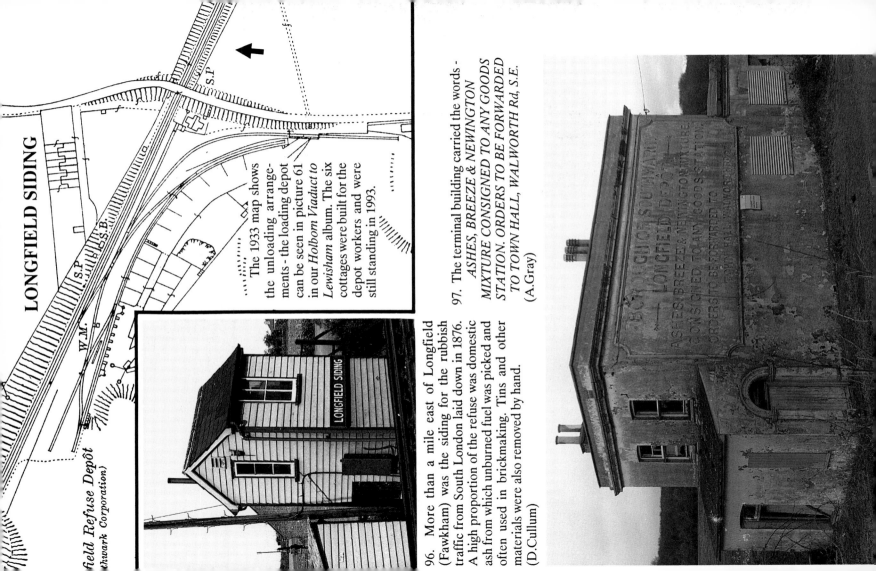

...field Refuse Depôt
...thwark Corporation)

The 1933 map shows the unloading arrangements - the loading depôt can be seen in picture 61 in our *Holborn Viaduct to Lewisham* album. The six cottages were built for the depot workers and were still standing in 1993.

96. More than a mile east of Longfield (Fawkham) was the siding for the rubbish traffic from South London laid down in 1876. A high proportion of the refuse was domestic ash from which unburned fuel was picked and often used in brickmaking. Tins and other materials were also removed by hand. (D.Cullum)

97. The terminal building carried the words - *ASHES, BREEZE & NEWINGTON MIXTURE CONSIGNED TO ANY GOODS STATION. ORDERS TO BE FORWARDED TO TOWN HALL, WALWORTH Rd, S.E.* (A.Gray)

98. The station opened on 6th May 1861, its name being pronounced *MEP-HAM*. A 1936 guide stated that Meopham was "a personable little township with green, windmill and stately church". The last was more than a mile south of the station. This 1923 view includes the cattle pens. (H.J.Patterson Rutherford)

L. C. & D. R.
Carnival & Lantern
Cycling Parade
RETURN
OCT. 5th, 1898.
Chatham
TO
MEOPHAM.
THIRD CLASS.
088
9d

L. C. & D. R.
Carnival & Lantern
Cycling Parade
TICKET.
OCT. 5th, 1898.
Meopham
TO
CHATHAM
THIRD CLASS.
088
9d

99. An express races towards the coast behind "King Arthur" class no.781 *Sir Aglovale* and approaches the final climb to the summit. The slender footbridge has more recently been replaced by a concrete structure further east. (D.Cullum coll.)

100. An example of the next generation of expresses is seen on Sunday 26th July 1953 as no.34066 *Spitfire* heads the 9.6am Victoria to Ramsgate. The signal box worked colour lights from 10th May 1959 and closed on 27th November 1965. (N.Sprinks)

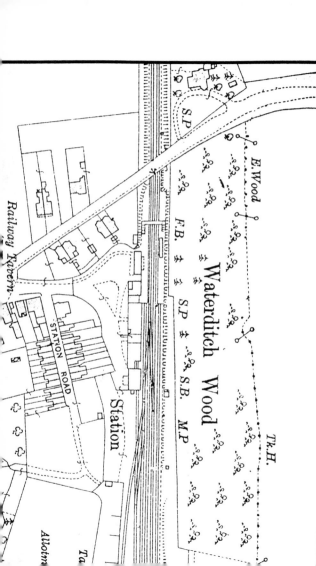

101. Not a person or car was in sight when the distant village was about 1200 when the lin... original buildings were recorded on 9th May opened and increased little over the succeed 1959 in total tranquility. The population of the ing 50 years. (D.Cullum)

The 1933 edition reveals that, while Kent was known as the "Garden of England", some locations could be termed the "Dustbin of London".

102. A 1992 view shows that the station had shrunk to a CLASP box while the former station house had been greatly improved, apart from the loss of the chimneys, important features of buildings of that era. The goods shed and yard had been replaced by a car park. (J.Scrace)

103. Goods facilities were withdrawn here on 2nd April 1962 but non-passenger trains continued to pass through. This one was operated by Rail Express Services on 5th May 1990 but was hauled by an all-grey departmental class 33, theoretically reserved for engineering purposes. (J.S.Petley)

S.P

Allotment Gar

opham Refuse Depôt
(Southwark Corporation)

SOLE STREET

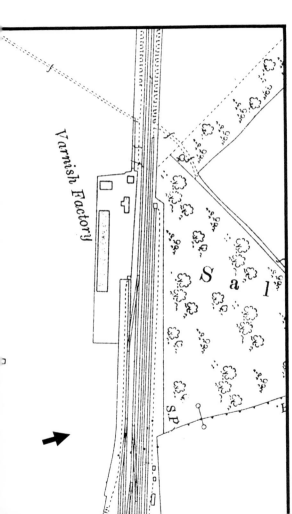

Varnish Factory

S   a   l

S.P.

104. Opened on 1st February 1861, the station served a sparsely populated area 300ft above sea level. Calling at 10.30am with the 9.4am (SO) Victoria to Chatham on 28th May 1938 is class E1 4-4-0 no. 1019. The signal box is obscured by steam and was closed on 16th July 1972, having worked colour lights since May 1959. (H.C.Casserley)

The varnish factory is only shown on this 1933 edition and as it has no road access it must be presumed that all goods inward and outward must have been over railway property.

Between here and Strood Junction small signal boxes had been situated at Cobham Bank (to 1934), Bush Bank (to about 1898) and Cuxton Road (to August 1968).

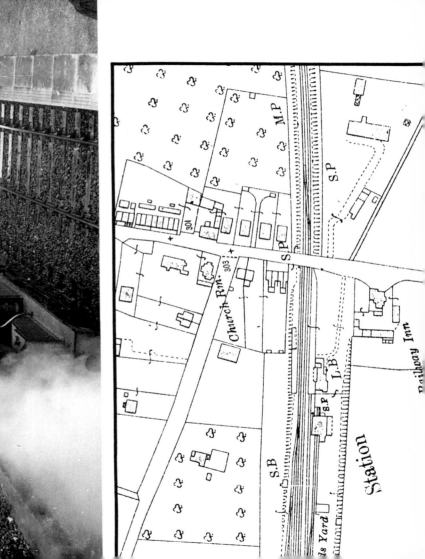

105. Departing at 9.1am on the same day is the 8.35 St.Mary Cray to Gillingham push-pull propelled by R class no. 1663. This had connected with the 7.48 Victoria to Sevenoaks Tubs Hill at St. Mary Cray. (H.C.Casserley)

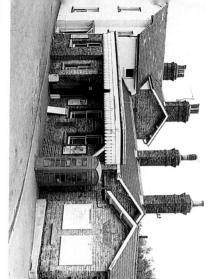

106. The footbridge was erected just prior to the 1939 electrification and made a good vantage point for the two previous photographs. Here we witness no. 34099 *Lynmouth* having topped the summit, which is near the rear of the 9.40am Victoria to Ramsgate on Sunday 20th June 1954. (N.Sprinks)

107. The buildings retained most of their original features, including their chimneys, when photographed in October 1986. Little had changed when this book was published seven years later. The booking hall doubled as a post office until 1975. A similar arrangement can be seen in picture no. 86 in our *Crawley to Littlehampton album.* (J.Scrace)

108. The goods yard closed on 19th April 1965 but a connection was maintained by the engineers. Their Permaquip tractor/personnel transporter and truck was photographed on 19th January 1993, along with their accommodation buildings. (M.Turvey)

ROCHESTER BRIDGE

The 1869 survey at 6" to 1 mile marked the LCDR main line from Sole Street curving on its steep descent from the chalk uplands on the top left part of the map. Top right is the tunnel carrying the SER's North Kent line from Gravesend. Strood station and Old Terminus are also marked. The line continues across the page and up the Medway Valley to Maidstone. There were no stations in Rochester at this time.

Illustrations and further details of Strood station can be found in our *Strood to Paddock Wood* album.

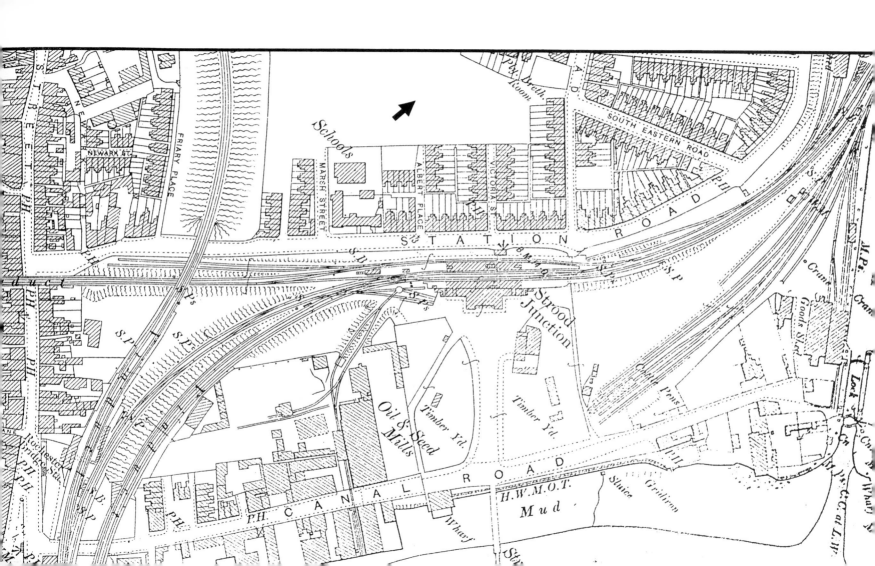

09. Strood is in the background of this picture f the three bridges, taken from Rochester Castle in 1899. During WWII the disused entre bridge was not only carrying double rail ack again but this was surrounded by timber ecking so that it could be used in the event of the adjacent road or rail bridges being damaged by enemy action. Conductor rails were stacked nearby and the bridge was ready by November 1942 but never used. More recently the abutments have been used for a new road bridge. (D.Cullum coll.)

Map labels: HIGHAM TUNNEL · STROOD DOCK · TO CHARING CROSS · S.E.R. · STROOD · TOOMER LOOP · ROCHESTER BRIDGE · TO VICTORIA · TO MAIDSTONE · R. MEDWAY · ROCHESTER COMMON · ROCHESTER BRIDGE · 1892 · FORT PITT TUNNEL · CHATHAM CENTRAL · TO CHATHAM · ROCHESTER · GOODS DEPOT · L.C. & D.R. · S.E.R. (CHATHAM CENTRAL LINE) · Cathedral

The 1909 edition has the former LCDR ain line across the bottom with a curving onnection to the ex-SER route at Strood unction. This link predates the LCDR main ne and was used initially by EKR trains. Their ock was conveyed to London Bridge by the ER. The link went out of use in 1860 depriving ochester and Chatham of the means of travel North Kent line stations, although goods affic continued. Mayor Toomer of Rochester ook the matter before the Railway Com- issioners and after prolonged wrangling a service recommenced on 1st April 1877. This curve was subsequently known as the "Toomer Loop". The intense rivalry between the two companies culminated in 1892 when the SER completed stations in Rochester, one of which it audaciously and erroneously called "Chatham Central". The first part of this route is marked *S.E.R. CHATHAM EXTENSION* and will be described more fully in a later album. At the bottom of the left page is Rochester Bridge station which was in use from December 1860 until 1st January 1917.

S.E.R. CHATHAM EXTENSION

Rochester Bridge

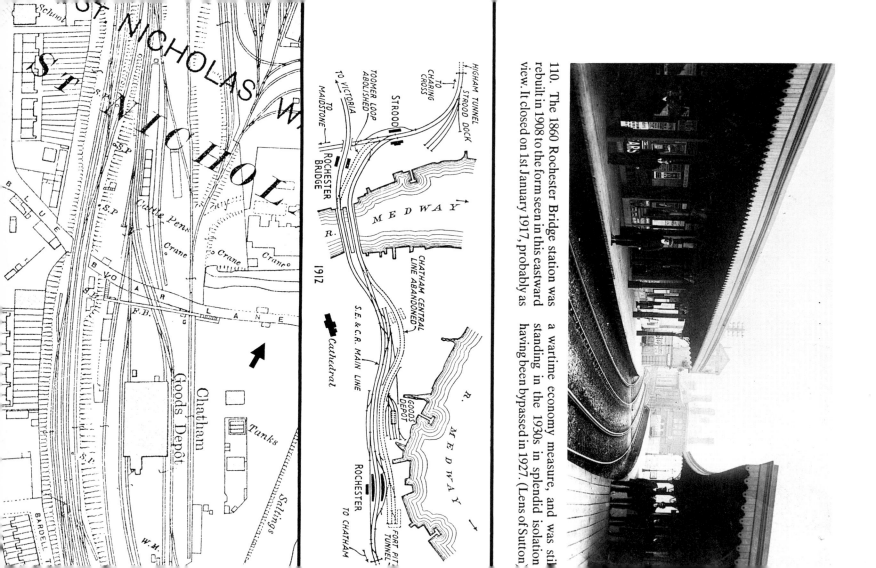

110. The 1860 Rochester Bridge station was rebuilt in 1908 to the form seen in this eastward view. It closed on 1st January 1917, probably as a wartime economy measure, and was still standing in the 1930s in splendid isolation having been bypassed in 1927. (Lens of Sutton)

11. A glimpse from a Victoria-bound train in January 1993 includes the Strood lines on the right. The Toomer Loop once passed to the left of the sub-station and Rochester Bridge station was on the other side of the train. (M.Turvey)

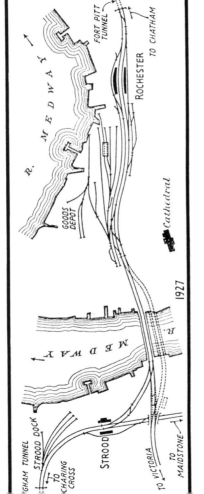

R. MEDWAY

FORT PITT TUNNEL

ROCHESTER

TO CHATHAM

GOODS DEPOT

Cathedral

1927

R. MEDWAY

STROOD DOCK

...GHAM TUNNEL

TO CHARING CROSS

STROOD

TO VICTORIA

TO MAIDSTONE

The need for competitive lines ceased in 1899, when the SECR was formed, but the Chatham Central line lingered on until 1911. Soon after this most of the line was abandoned, as was the Toomer Loop, but both bridges were retained. The decking of the ex-SER bridge was damaged by fire on 29th June 1919 and so the Toomer Loop was reinstated until 19th January 1922. In 1927 the ex-LCDR bridge was abandoned and the bridge over the Maidstone Line rebuilt and realigned, reducing the main line curvature. This 1932 survey has very little evidence of the former SER route, the terminus of which had been close to the High Street (right). On the left is a trailing connection to Chatham Goods Depot (ex-LCDR) and on the right page is Rochester station, but Fort Pitt Tunnels is just off the page. The diagrams are from the 1935 Railway Magazine.

112. The station was opened on 1st March 1893 to compete with the nearby SER Chatham Central which came into use exactly twelve months earlier. The quadruple track and four platforms came into use in 191_ following the closure of the former SER_ terminus. (H.J.Patterson Rutherford)

113. A second picture from 28th March 1914 shows a train from Chatham emerging from Fort Pitt Tunnel, which is 428 yds long. The locomotive is class M3 4-4-0 no. 476 which was built at the LCDR's Longhedge Works in 189_ and was scrapped in 1927. (H.J.Patterson Rutherford)

115. The ground level buildings appear to date from 1893 and were not altered significantly at the time of the quadrupling in 1911. Local attractions include the castle and cathedral, both visible in the next picture. (Lens of Sutton)

114. A photograph from 30th June 1934 features class B1 4-4-0 no.1441 with a "Birdcage" coach, so called on account of the guards lookout which was a distinctive feature of the SECR. The sailor is probably not travelling first class officially. (H.C.Casserley)

116. New platform slabs and improvements to the canopies are in progress on 28th March 1953 as the 12.45pm (SO) Cannon Street to Ramsgate passes through, first stop Chatham at 1.31. It is hauled by no.34100 *Appledore* and class L1 no. 31755 is waiting with empty stock. (R.C.Riley)

117. A glimpse of the goods yard is obtained on 10th May 1958 as class L 4-4-0 no. 31781 works more empty stock and a 4EPB arrives, bound for Gillingham, then the end of the conductor rail. (A.E.Bennett)

118. A snap from August 1958 includes the new signal box under construction, a London train proceeding in a cloud of exhaust steam, an LMS-type 2-6-2T at the top of the incline to the goods yard and a brake van parked on it. (P.J.Tyrell)

119. The 1912 box (right) was superseded by a panel in this new building on 10th May 1959. It took over the main line work of Strood Box on 10th September 1971. Another local closure took place on 10th July 1927 when Rochester Junction ceased to function. This box was between the two sets of tracks at the east end of the bridges. (J.J.Smith)

120. A westward view from the up platform on 19th January 1993 reveals that the former goods yard area had become a haven for weeds, and that the long lattice footbridge adjacent to Blue Boar Lane still spanned the site. Approaching is the 11.57 Charing Cross to Gillingham which is passing the panel box and the electrified loop. The basic service was then two stopping trains per hour to Victoria and two to Charing Cross, platforms 1 and 4 being used for extras in peak hours. From May 1993, the half-hourly fast trains to Victoria also stopped at Rochester, reflecting its growing importance as a tourist centre. (M.Turvey)

MP Middleton Press

EVOLVING THE ULTIMATE RAIL ENCYCLOPEDIA

OOP Out of Print at time of printing - Please check current availability · BROCHURE AVAILABLE SHOWING NEW TITLES

Easebourne Lane, Midhurst, West Sussex. GU29 9AZ Tel:01730 813169
www.middletonpress.co.uk email:info@middletonpress.co.uk

A-0 906520   B-1 873793   C-1 901706   D-1 904474